DK Eye Wonder

Volcano

LONDON, NEW YORK, MUNICH,
MELBOURNE, and DELHI

Written and edited by Lisa Magloff
Designed by Laura Roberts

Publishing manager Susan Leonard
Managing art editor Clare Shedden
Jacket design Chris Drew
Picture researcher Sarah Pownall
Production Shivani Pandey
DTP Designer Almudena Díaz
Consultant Chris Pellant

First published in Great Britain in 2003 by
Dorling Kindersley Limited
80 Strand, London WC2R 0RL

4 6 8 10 9 7 5 3

A CIP catalogue record for this book
is available from the British Library.

ISBN 0-7513-6768-0

Colour reproduction by Colourscan, Singapore
Printed and bound in Italy by L.E.G.O.

see our complete
catalogue at
www.dk.com

Contents

Spitting fire

Deep inside the Earth, rocks melt into a thick liquid called magma. When the pressure in the Earth's crust builds up, it is magma that explodes out in a volcanic eruption.

As it rises, the magma breaks up rocks near the surface, which can cause earthquakes.

Hot rocks

The red-hot molten rock that explodes out of a volcano is beautiful but deadly. It is so hot that it can melt steel.

Once it has risen to the surface, magma is called lava.

Earth's crust

The Earth's crust is made of...

Loose rocks and dirt.

Sedimentary rocks made from bits of rock squashed together.

Igneous rocks made from magma that has cooled.

Metamorphic rock made from squashed rocks.

Ready to blow

The force of an exploding volcano can throw lava more than 610 metres (2,000 feet) into the air. Ash can be thrown up to 25 miles (40 km) high!

The Earth's crust is a layer of rock between 5.6 and 68 km (3.5 and 42 miles) thick.

lower mantle

outer core

inner core

The layer of moving rock below the crust is the mantle.

Peeling away the layers

The Earth is made up of many layers, just like an onion. Instead of onion skin, the Earth's layers are made of rock and metals.

Deep in the Earth

Below the mantle is the outer core. This layer is made up of iron and nickel that has melted. Below this is the inner core, where temperatures reach 4,500 °C (8,132 °F).

Jigsaw Earth

The Earth's crust is broken into pieces called plates, which are always moving. Sometimes we can feel the movement in an earthquake. Many volcanoes occur in places where plates bump together or pull apart.

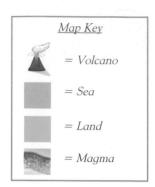

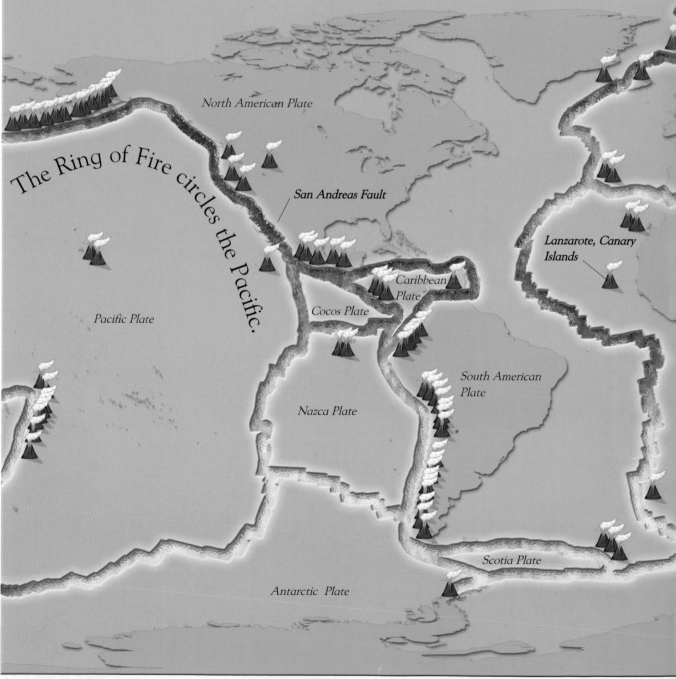

North American Plate

The Ring of Fire circles the Pacific.

San Andreas Fault

Lanzarote, Canary Islands

Caribbean Plate

Cocos Plate

Pacific Plate

Nazca Plate

South American Plate

Scotia Plate

Antarctic Plate

Visible fault

The San Andreas Fault, in California, USA, is a place where two plates slide against each other. The plates move about 1 cm (0.5 in) a year.

All in a row

On Lanzarote, Canary Islands, magma bubbles up in places where plates break apart. These weak spots are called fissures.

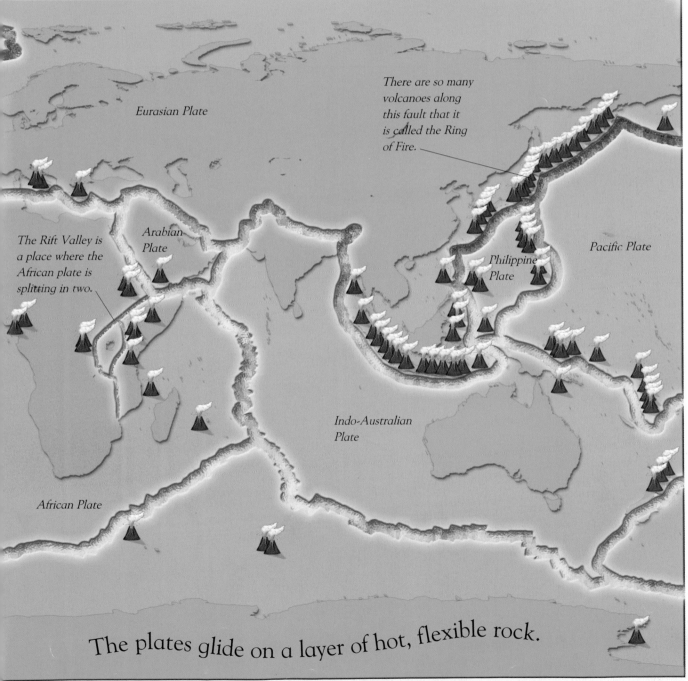

Eurasian Plate

There are so many volcanoes along this fault that it is called the Ring of Fire.

Arabian Plate

The Rift Valley is a place where the African plate is splitting in two.

Pacific Plate

Philippine Plate

Indo-Australian Plate

African Plate

The plates glide on a layer of hot, flexible rock.

Hot spots

In some places, the Earth's crust is thin enough for a column of hot magma to burn a hole and create a volcano. These places are called hot spots.

Hot water spot

Yellowstone Park in Wyoming, USA, is located over a hot spot. Two million years ago a volcano erupted here. Today, underground heat fuels the park's 10,000 geysers.

Lava erupts from Piton de la Fournaise in many places at the same time.

Island of fire

Réunion Island, in the Indian Ocean, contains one of the world's most active volcanoes – Piton de la Fournaise. Réunion Island formed over a hot spot about 5 million years ago.

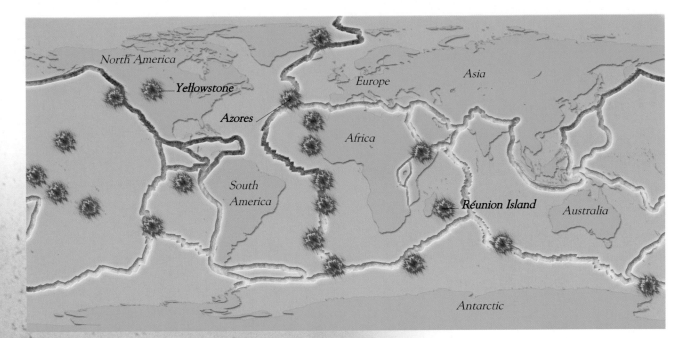

North America
Yellowstone
Europe
Asia
Azores
Africa
South
America
Réunion Island
Australia
Antarctic

In the ocean

The thin plates at the bottom of the sea are most easily pierced by hot magma. When this happens, an island is formed over the hot spot.

 Plate line   Hot spot

Underground oven

The Azores islands lie over a hot spot in the Atlantic Ocean. People here take advantage of the free underground heat and use it to cook their food.

This pot contains dinner for an Azores family.

Red-hot rivers

When a volcano erupts, hot liquid rock either explodes outwards, or flows onto the Earth. Once it is outside the volcano, the liquid rock can cause a lot of damage.

Exploding out

Sometimes, the liquid rock is under a lot of pressure underground. When this happens, the lava spurts or explodes out of the volcano.

Destructive heat

Hot, liquid lava spreads out into rivers that can cover the countryside before it cools. It burns anything in its path, even roads.

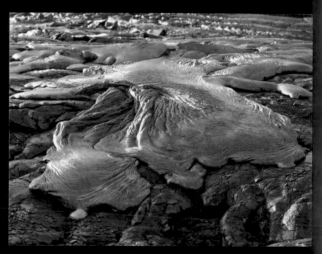

Slow but steady

When lava seeps out of the ground rather than explodes, it travels very slowly. Flowing lava is easier to run away from than exploding lava, but it is just as destructive to the landscape.

Aa and Pahoehoe

There are many types of lava. Aa lava moves quickly and hardens to form sharp chunks. Pahoehoe lava moves slowly and often forms smooth rock when it hardens.

Pahoehoe lava flows grow a smooth skin.

Aa rock is covered in sharp chunks and is difficult to walk over once it has cooled.

As lava cools, it forms a hard "skin" over the liquid flow.

Lava facts

● The temperature of some lava is seven to twelve times hotter than boiling water.

● The words aa and pahoehoe come from the Hawaiian language.

● Lava can form many different shapes, such as cones, tubes, and even hair!

Glowing river

This intensely hot aa lava flow glows brightly. As it cools, the flow slows down and thickens, but since it cools very slowly, it can cover hundreds of kilometres before it stops.

Deadly blast

When a volcano explodes, gases inside the earth escape with so much force that the lava is blasted into billions of tiny pieces. These pieces of rock come in all sizes, from huge boulders to fine dust.

Amongst this cloud of ash there may be pieces of rock, gravel, and dust.

Steamy beginning

Steam can sometimes be seen escaping from the top or sides of a volcano. This is often the first sign that a volcano is active or may be getting ready to erupt.

Poisonous gas

Rocks and lava are dangerous, but the most deadly types of eruptions spew out tonnes of ash and poisonous gases that can cause death by suffocation.

No swimming!

Gases inside a volcano can also seep out slowly into lakes on the top or sides of the volcano. The gases can turn the lakes into pools of burning acid that dissolve skin and bone.

The school run

Sakurajima volcano, in Japan, hurls lava rocks down onto the nearby town almost every day. For their protection, all the children on the island are required by law to wear hard hats to and from school.

The large rocks that are hurled from volcanoes are called bombs. Some bombs are as large as a house.

A gritty tale

Many forms of magma can be thrown from a volcano. Pumice is full of tiny bubbles of gas and is light enough to float. Smaller pieces are the size of gravel or dust.

Bomb

Gravel

Dust

Pumice

Volcanic weather

When a volcano erupts, huge amounts of dust and ash are thrown high up into the atmosphere. This debris can affect the weather all over the world, blocking out sunlight and turning summer days cold.

Travelling ash

This satellite photo was taken in 1991, one month after Mt. Pinatubo erupted in the Philippines. The light areas show the ash and dust from the volcano. It had already spread all around the world.

The eruption of Mt. Pinatubo lowered world temperatures by 0.5°C (1°F) for one year.

Lightning strikes

Lightning is often seen during eruptions. It is caused by tiny pieces of lava in an ash cloud rubbing against each other. The rubbing creates an electrical charge, which is lightning.

Turning day to night
When Mt Pinatubo erupted, clouds of ash 40 km (25 miles) high blocked out the Sun. The land was dark and covered with grey ash.

In hot water

Water that is trapped underground near a volcano can get very hot. Sometimes, the water turns into steam and shoots into the air as a geyser. At other times, it seeps up in pools called hot springs.

The water inside a geyser can be as much as three times hotter than water boiling in a kettle.

A rainbow of colours
This is the Fly Geyser in Nevada, USA. The red cones formed when liquid minerals in the hot water cooled and turned solid. The yellow and green colours come from algae that live in the water.

Glorious mud

Underground heat from a volcano can even boil mud. This mud is rich in minerals and is often collected and used as a skin treatment. People bathe in the mud to make their skin soft and smooth.

Old Faithful

One of the most popular geysers in the world is Old Faithful in Yellowstone National Park, USA. This geyser spurts faithfully every 78 minutes or so.

Old Faithful shoots water between 30 and 50 m (98 – 165 feet) into the air.

Fire under the sea

Under the sea, hot magma, chemicals, and minerals burn their way through thin spots in the Earth's plates. The lava and minerals bubble up to make islands and other unusual homes for undersea life.

Studying a hot subject
When lava erupts in the water, it moves slowly and cools quickly. Scientists study underwater lava flows to learn more about how islands form.

LAVA DIVING
Because magma cools down very quickly underwater, experienced SCUBA divers can sometimes get a close-up look at small, undersea eruptions.

Underwater chimneys

The minerals that rise to the ocean floor from deep in the Earth quickly harden and make a chimney shape. These chimneys are called black smokers. Many unusual animals live in the warm, mineral waters.

Black smoker facts

- Most black smokers are very deep – more than 2 km (1 mile) below the surface.

- The first black smoker was discovered in 1977.

- The animals living near black smokers include mussels, clams, and crabs.

Living on a chimney

Colourful tube worms live around black smokers. Special bacteria live inside these worms. They change the chemicals pouring out of the smokers into food.

The volcanic seabed

Scientists believe there may be as many as 20,000 volcanoes under the sea. That's more than 90 per cent of all the volcanoes on the planet. Many of the Earth's islands were formed from these undersea volcanoes.

This crab has made its home on the tube worms.

This extinct volcano has stopped erupting.

An active volcano about to erupt under the ocean floor.

Birth of an island

When a volcano erupts deep under the sea, the lava piles up instead of flowing away. If the eruptions continue, the lava gradually builds up, until one day it breaks the surface and forms an island.

An island's birthday

In 1963, fishermen near Iceland saw a new island rise out of the water. The island was named Surtsey, after Surtur, the ancient Norse god of fire.

Three years later...

Once the lava flows stopped, plants and animals began to find their way to the new island. After just a few years, Surtsey was home to birds, grasses, and seals.

It takes millions of years for a volcano to reach the surface and become an island.

Underwater laboratory

As a new volcano grows towards the surface, it provides a home for a wide variety of marine life. This is why growing volcanoes are a great place to study undersea life.

Islands may look large, but they are only a tiny bit of the whole volcano.

Home sweet home

The Galapagos Islands, in the Pacific Ocean, are volcanic islands that broke the surface of the water about four million years ago. Since that time, many types of animals and plants have come to live on the islands.

Tsunami

Many coastal towns' worst dread is a tsunami – a huge wave that destroys everything in its path. Many tsunamis are caused by eruptions.

Making waves
When a volcano erupts under the sea, large parts of the ocean floor are lifted up, displacing water and creating a wave.

Landslide danger
Tsunamis are also caused when a large eruption sends huge amounts of lava and mud tumbling into the ocean.

At first, the displaced water is almost invisible as it travels quickly towards shore.

A tsunami starts when a volcano erupts on the ocean floor.

Far out at sea, lava deep inside the Earth rises to the surface.

Tsunamis can travel up to 805 kph (500 mph) at sea.

Dangerous wave

Tsunamis can be even more dangerous than the eruptions that cause them. One of the deadliest tsunamis of all time was caused by the eruption of Krakatau, in Indonesia, in 1883. The lava and gas killed few people, but the tsunami killed over 36,000.

City threatened

Huge tsunamis can sweep away entire towns and villages, flood hundreds of metres inland and strip away beaches and vegetation.

When the tsunami reaches shallow water, it swells upwards, forming a huge wave.

Water travelling back from the shore is also sucked up into the wave. A towering and terrifying tsunami is about to hit land!

Tsunami facts

● On 21 May 1792, Unzen volcano caused a tsunami that killed 14,300 people.

● The tallest recorded tsunami was 85 m (279 feet) high.

● The word tsunami means "harbour wave" in Japanese.

Dead or alive?

Some volcanoes can seem to be dead, but they are only sleeping. A volcano that is not erupting, but might erupt again, is called dormant. A volcano that cannot erupt any more is called extinct.

In the shadow of Mt. Fuji
Mt. Fuji, in Japan, has been dormant since 1770, but could come to life again at any time. This would be devastating for the 12 million people of Tokyo – 97 km (60 miles) away.

Out of the blue
Mt. Pinatubo, in the Philippines, erupted in 1991 after lying dormant for 400 years. Ash and gas flowed along the ground faster than a car. The driver of this blue truck had to really put his foot down to escape.

WAKING UP
Mt. Pinatubo began waking up in April 1991, when people heard rumbling sounds and saw steam and ash coming from the sides of the volcano. More than 200,000 people were quickly evacuated from the area. The volcano finally erupted on July 15.

Starting to wake up

Scientists use satellites to keep a close watch on dormant volcanoes. The dots on these photos of Chiliques volcano, in Chile, show where magma is rising as the volcano wakes up.

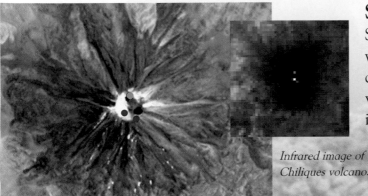

Infrared image of Chiliques volcano.

Satellite image of Chiliques volcano.

On solid ground

This church in Le Puy, France, was built on the remains of an old volcano. The volcano is extinct and will never erupt again.

Living in fear

Mount Etna, in Italy, is Europe's largest and most active volcano. The volcano has erupted at least 190 times in 3,500 years, but even so, thousands of people live and work on its slopes.

Blast from the past
One of the most dramatic eruptions of Mt. Etna was in 1669. Fifteen villages around the volcano were buried by lava, but no one was killed.

A pet's sixth sense
Some people who live near Mt. Etna watch the behaviour of their pet cats to try and predict eruptions. Cats are very sensitive to changes in pressure that occur just before an eruption.

A constant threat

When Mt. Etna erupted in 2002, people living near the volcano had to evacuate their homes as the lava got close.

Early warning systems around Mt. Etna help people escape in time.

Build a barrier

The people living near Mt. Etna build barriers to help divert the flow of lava away from populated areas. During the 1669 eruption, the people of one town used rocks to divert the lava. Today, mechanical diggers are used.

Luckily, Mt. Etna's lava flows very slowly.

Lava-land

There are more than 200 volcanoes in Iceland, which is over a large hot spot in the Earth's crust. In January 1973, Eldfell volcano, on the island of Heimaey, erupted. The eruption continued for six months.

Eldfell means "fire mountain" in Icelandic. This fire mountain buried or destroyed more than 370 buildings.

A curtain of fire

During the eruption of Eldfell, lava fountains spurted up from cracks in the volcano and formed a curtain of fire. Seawater was used to cool the lava and slow down the flow.

Buried homes

Most of Heimaey's 5,300 inhabitants were taken to Iceland's mainland and so escaped the eruption. However, most of the island's buildings were buried in black ash. Many of the buildings were later dug out and restored.

A natural heat

The heat from Iceland's many volcanoes is put to good use. People bathe and relax in hot pools like this one, while the nearby power plant uses the heat from the water to make electricity.

Mount Saint Helens

One of the best-studied eruptions of all time occurred on 18 May 1980. That morning, Mt. St Helens, in the state of Washington, USA, exploded in a fury of ash and smoke while scientists nearby took measurements.

Before 1980 eruption.

After 1980 eruption.

Blowing its top

Before the eruption, Mt. St Helens had a beautiful snow-capped peak. The blast tore off most of the north side of the volcano and left a huge, gaping hole big enough to fit an entire city into. This was the first time scientists had ever watched a volcano erupt from its side.

Huge explosion

Rocks, ash, volcanic gas, and steam blasted upwards and outwards faster than a jet plane and hotter than a furnace. Ash rose 24 km (15 miles) into the atmosphere in just 15 minutes.

The top 400 metres (1,312 feet) of Mt. St Helens was blasted away.

A dreadful aftermath
The blast killed 57 people, destroyed wildlife and river valleys, and knocked down enough trees to build 300,000 homes.

A bottle of ash, please!
Ash from the eruption blocked out the sunlight for 400 km (250 miles) around. Later, the ash was bottled up and sold as a souvenir.

Montserrat

Tiny Montserrat island in the West Indies was very peaceful until 1995. That year, Soufriere Hills volcano began erupting. Since then, most of the residents have had to flee the island for their lives.

Buried and deserted

In December 1997, Montserrat's capital city, Plymouth, was buried in 2 metres (6 feet) of mud and ash.

Paradise lost

Monserrat was once a popular vacation and tourist spot. Today, the airport is buried under ash, and any tourists must arrive by ferry.

Time to re-build?

Scientists do not know when the people of Montserrat will be able to completely rebuild their island. Small eruptions and lava flows continue today.

Squeezed out

The people of Montserrat are being squeezed into smaller and smaller parts of their island as the volcano takes over. Only a small area of the island is now safe.

Plymouth, former capital city.

This area is the only part considered safe to live on.

Montserrat facts

- Around 8,000 people, two-thirds of the population, have left the island.

- Scientists think the Soufriere Hills volcano is about 100,000 years old.

- Since 1995, the eruptions have killed 20 people.

Land of fire

Indonesia lies in between two large plates. It is home to over 125 active volcanoes and more recorded eruptions than any other country. Many of Indonesia's 15,000 islands were formed by volcanic activity.

Big bang
When Krakatau volcano erupted in 1883, the explosion was heard 4,000 km (2,400 miles) away at Alice Springs in Australia.

A beauty and a beast
Tengger Caldera is one of Indonesia's most visited volcanic areas. Its beauty masks a fiery heart – there have been more than 50 eruptions here in the last 200 years.

Mt. Bromo

Mt. Batok

Sulphur mining
Indonesia's many eruptions have brought valuable minerals close to the surface, where they are easy to mine. This man is carrying rocks of sulphur.

Since 1967, more than 600 people have been killed by Mt. Semeru.

Mt. Semeru

THE OGRE'S TASK

Legend says that Mt. Bromo was created when an ogre was ordered to dig a trench to win the hand of a princess. When the princess's angry father saw that the ogre might finish the trench, he ordered the ogre to speed up. The ogre died of exhaustion, and the half-coconut he used to dig the trench became Mt. Bromo.

Ancient tragedy

On the morning of 24 August, 79 AD, Mt. Vesuvius, in Italy, erupted. Hot ash, dust, lava, and clouds of deadly gas rained down on the people of Pompeii and Herculaneum, burying both towns for 1600 years.

Preserved in ash

Pompeii is so well-preserved that it provides us with good evidence of everyday life in an ancient Roman town. Archaeologists can even read the graffiti on the town's walls.

A Pompeiian victim

This man suffocated in the smoke and ash of the eruption. His body later decayed to leave a hole. In modern times, the hole was filled with plaster to make a cast.

Sleeping, but not dead

Today, Mt. Vesuvius may look quiet, but the volcano has erupted about 36 times since 79 AD. The most recent eruption was in 1944 and lasted for 10 days. That time, only a few people were hurt.

This dog suffocated while chained to a post.

Died on duty

This is a cast of a dog that died while he was guarding the house of his owner, a man named Vesonius Primus.

This man tried to shield his face from the ash.

This is a plaster cast of a dog that died in the eruption.

Working in the hot zone

A scientist who studies volcanoes is called a volcanologist. For these scientists, research can get pretty hot. In order to collect information about volcanoes, they must get close to a volcano's fiery interior.

Suited and booted

In order for volcanologists to pick up burning rock samples and walk across red-hot lava, they need to wear a special suit and heat-proof boots.

The silver suit reflects the heat of the volcano and leaves the person inside cool.

DANGEROUS WORK

When volcanologists work around an active volcano, if there is any warning of an eruption or violent activity, they usually leave. Unfortunately, sometimes the activity changes quickly and there is little or no warning. Between 1975 and 2001, 29 volcanologists died while studying volcanoes.

This camera will provide scientists with a close up view of the inside of the crater.

Robot on a mission

The Dante robot is sent into volcanoes to gather information where it is too dangerous for people to go. One day it will be used to study volcanoes on other planets.

These volcanologists are taking samples of gas. The gas may give clues as to when the volcano will next erupt.

Deadly gases

Even if it is not too hot, there may be invisible dangers in the form of deadly gases seeping from below ground. This is why gas masks are required uniform for volcanologists.

Visiting volcanoes

Volcanoes are fascinating, and many people will go a long way to visit them. Each year, thousands of tourists travel to active volcanoes for the opportunity to get up close and personal with boiling lava.

Popular volcanoes

- Kilauea volcano has been erupting since 1982.

- Yasur volcano in Vanuatu has erupted 10-20 times each hour for 800 years.

- Tourists to White Island volcano in New Zealand can walk right inside the crater.

It's safer up here

Some volcanoes can only be safely visited from the air. Hot lava and poisonous gases make it too dangerous to get any closer. These volcanoes are best toured by helicopter.

Stationary pool of hot lava.

A spectacular display

Forget fireworks! A volcanic sound and light show beats them all! This volcano in Hawaii has a small eruption almost every night and people hike for several kilometres to watch it.

It is even possible to camp overnight near this active volcano in Hawaii.

VOLCANO PARK

Volcanoes National Park, on the island of Hawaii, contains one of the most active volcanoes in the world – Kilauea. Every year, thousands of tourists visit the volcano, which has been erupting since 1983.

Weird and wonderful

Lava flows can form a large variety
of weird and wonderful shapes when
they cool. Sometimes, even scientists
cannot explain how all these
fantastic features were created!

Towering cones of lava
These structures in Pinnacles
National Park, California,
USA, were formed 7,700 years
ago by lava erupting from
nearby Mt. Mazama.

Chimney houses

Hundreds of years ago, people hollowed out these volcanic chimneys in Cappadocia, Turkey, and used them as houses. People still live in some of them.

A road for giants

The people of ancient Ireland believed these rocks were the work of a giant named Finn McCool. The Giants Causeway was actually created 60 million years ago by cooling lava flows.

Cold monkeys

These Japanese monkeys have learned that a soak in a nearby volcanic hot spring makes a nice break from the winter chill and helps them to stay clean.

Animals also enjoy unusual volcanic areas.

Out of the ashes

A volcanic eruption can bring devastation, but it can also bring renewal. The burning lava clears out old, dead plants, while the ash that settles on the land makes a great fertilizer for new plants.

Life returns

A few years after an eruption, plant life has returned to this volcano. Plants grow back fastest when there is a lot of ash.

First growth

Ferns are some of the first plants to grow after an eruption. They have very tough seeds and are able to push their way up through solid lava.

Fertile slopes

Farmers near this volcano in Indonesia take advantage of the fertile volcanic ash by growing their crops right up the sides and into the crater of the volcano.

Making a meal of it

Without volcanoes, many people who live in some of the poorest places in the world would struggle to grow enough food. The ash makes poor farm land fertile enough to feed everyone.

Glossary

Here are the meanings of some words that are useful to know when learning about volcanoes.

Aa lava a crumbly, lumpy type of lava that moves slowly and can form tall flows.

Algae small, simple plants that live in water.

Ash very small, fine particles of lava that can block out sunlight.

Bacteria microscopic animals that can get their energy from chemicals.

Basalt the most common kind of volcanic rock, made from very runny lava.

Black smoker volcanic vent on the sea floor that belches out hot minerals.

Bomb big blob of lava thrown out by a volcano, which cools in mid-air.

Chemical a natural substance made when different types of atoms combine together.

Core the metallic centre of the Earth.

Crater the part of a volcano that connects to the main chimney and out of which lava and ash erupts.

Crater lake a lake formed in the crater of a volcano.

Crust the hard, outer layer of the Earth.

Dormant a volcano that has not erupted for a long time, but could erupt again.

Eruption when lava, ash, or gas explodes out of a volcano.

Extinct a volcano that cannot ever erupt again.

Fault a crack in the Earth's crust where rocks have moved.

Fissure a crack in the ground which runny lava oozes out of.

Geyser a place where underground water, heated by magma, spurts into the air.

Hot spot a place where rising magma burns through the Earth's crust.

Hot spring a place where hot water from under the ground bubbles to the surface.

Landslide the sliding of loose earth and rock down a steep slope.

Lava the name for magma that has erupted to the surface.

Magma rock deep in the Earth that has melted to a liquid.

Mantle the part of the Earth's interior that lies in between the crust and the core.

Metamorphic rock rock formed from other rocks that are under intense heat and pressure.

Mineral a natural substance that is not a plant or animal.

Mud pot a pool of hot, boiling mud.

Pahoehoe lava a hot, runny lava that moves freely in shallow flows.

Plate the moving part of the mantle and crust.

Rift a place where two plates are pulling apart to create a crack in the crust.

Ring of Fire an area in the Pacific Ocean that includes many of the world's most active and violent volcanoes.

Seismograph a machine which measures the movement of the Earth's surface.

Tsunami a destructive sea wave that can be caused by a volcanic eruption.

Volcanologist a scientist who studies volcanoes.

Index

Useful websites

http://volcano.und.nodak.edu/vw.html
Loads of information about volcanoes all over the world, along with features explaining how volcanoes work.

http://vulcan.wr.usgs.gov
USA government Cascades Volcano Observatory site. Photos, information, kids friends volcano FAQs.

Acknowledgements

Dorling Kindersley would like to thank:
Colin Bowler of Alan Collinson Design/Geo-Innovations, for map design, and Louise Halsey for her original volcano illustrations. Thanks, also, to the following DK staff: Jacqueline Gooden, Elinor Greenwood, Lorrie Mack, Fleur Star, Cheryl Telfer, and Sadie Thomas.

Picture credits

The publisher would like to thank the following for their kind permission to reproduce their photographs / images:
a=above; c=centre; b=below; l=left; r=right; t=top;

Mario Cipollini: 27tl. **Bruce Coleman Inc:** Stella Sneered 20cr. **Corbis:** 26-27c; Yann Arthus-Bertrand 43b, 44-45; Dan Bool/Sygma 34-35; Gary Braasch 31br; Carol Cohen 44c; Sergio Dorantes 34tr; Chris Hellier 43tl; Ted Horowitz 44l; Michael S. Lewis 8tr; Ludovic Maisant 13tr; Pat O'Hara 42, 48; Robert Patrick 32tr, 32bl; Roger Ressmeyer 13c, 20bl, 36-37b, 39b, 40bl, 41b, 41t; Hans Georg Roth 9br; Royalty-Free Images 24tr; Sean Sexton 37cr; Strauss/Curtis 45br; Kevin Schafer 44bl; Hans Strand 29cr; James A Sugar 31r; Nick Wheeler 22c; Ralph White 19cr; Adam Woolfit 25cr. **Ecoscene:** Wayne Lawler 48c. **Lin Esposito:** 36c. **GeoScience Features Picture Library:** 20tl. **Getty Images:** Warren Bolster 22-23c; Michael Dunning 22tr; Jack Dykinga 16-17; G. Brad Lewis 10cr; 46-47; NASA 21c; Guido Alberto Rossi 12cl; Schafer & Hill 22l; Pete Turner 28-29, 29tr; Greg Vaughn 2-3; Art Wolfe 12-13c. **Robert Harding Picture Library:** 10tr, 10cl, 11, Photri 30cl; E. Simanor 43tr. **Katz/FSP:** 14cl, 24-25; R. Gaillarde/Gamma 8-9. **NASA:** 5tr, 25tl, 25tc, 33tr. **Panos Pictures:** Rob Huibers 32-33. **Chris and Helen Pellant:** 17tl. **Popperfoto:** Tony Gentile/Reuters 1; Reuteurs 38. **Powerstock Photolibrary:** Superstock 13br. **Rex Features:** Sipa Press 15. **Science Photo Library:** 30-31; Bernhard Edmaier 2tc, 4-5c, 7tr, 34bl; NASA/Carnegie Mellon University 39tr; Mark Newman 14bc; David Parker 7tl. **Seapics.com:** Doug Perrine 18. **Verena Tunnicliffe:** 19tr. **US Geological Survey:** Lyn Topinka, United States Department of the Interior, U.S Geological Survey, David A. Johnston Cascades Volcano Observatory, Vancouver, Washington 30cr.